Breathing in and Breathing out

Building Relationships with yourself and others Volume 2

By Doris Richardson-Edsell

Dedicated to authors Robert Dembik and William West, PhD., for their wonderful inspiration

To Maureen Roos for her belief in my abilities as an inspirational author

I have skill at growing plants; you water them, feed them and they flourish throughout the season.

In love; although I have had many experiences; they do not always flourish as my plants do!

Table of Contents

Breathing in and breathing out

There is much information on the many benefits of meditation, and learning how to breathe; slowing yourself down and becoming centered and balanced in your life is worth exploring.

Meditation helps you to know your authentic self; digging deep into your spirit and finding that soft spot of love, balance and harmony.

Begin with some relaxation; lying down, putting your hands on your lower belly and feeling the rise and fall of your deep *ocean breaths* that slow down on your command.

You are in control; you do not have to do anything perfect; just be with this moment in time, feeling the rise and fall of your belly; breathing in through your nose for the slow count of 5, holding your breath for a second, and then breathing out through your nose again for the count of 7.

This moment can be your first step toward the deepness of meditation. Breathing allows you to practice slowing everything down and just being.

You are not planning your next vacation; you are just planning your next breath.

Just a ride in the country

I was riding my bike on a country road and spotted a deer

The deer was prancing and dancing, stopped at a beautiful meadow and took a look at me, surrounded by beautiful green and yellow grass that swayed with the summer breeze. I thought it was just coincidental until he started to run along the side of me as I road my bike like he was riding along. It was a moment in time; especially when he stayed along side of me, he did it 3 times, so I had to think he was trying to play with me and the colors and beauty of the deer froze me into the moment. I could not think of anything else for quite some time that day. All I could think is *wishing I had my camera because no one will believe this one.* And then I thought I will express myself with this beautiful moment by exploring some painting (something I have not done in a long time). But ever since the deer, I feel more in touch with nature and the beauty of colors.

Find your way in nature and its beauty

Breathing in some warm colors can soften your mood

Circles of energy surround and heal your life

Circling around, just like the energy in circles themselves; the deer found that his path was with me for the moment in time.

You too make circles in your life with the energy that you have in your soul. It circles with movements that you make; especially during exercise; even passive exercise such as Tai-chi and yoga where you find you center and balance. And when you meditate; you also find that your energy center can calm you; allowing your breathing to slow down.

Your eyes begin to close; but you are awake, finding your own special brand of harmony inside.

It is like a sweet melody softly tickling you with a feather that caresses your life. And when you finish your practice; the calmness of the moment is yours to keep throughout the day.

Find your peace in life through nature, practicing meditation; breathing in and breathing out wonderful colors that help you stay in a calm, loving way.

Successful living

There are many people who believe that if you work at something hard and long enough, success will come.

That is true about some things such as studying for an exam, but in real life events, you may have to give up the attempt at mending a personal relationship or your family relations and concentrate on mending yourself.

Many authors speak on the topic of mending broken people, but how do you know if something is too broken to fix?

When *Humpty Dumpty* fell off the wall, his great fall took a lot of people to try and put him back together, and they gave up; Humpty was too broken to fix.

And even if you have a village supporting your efforts, you may not be able to fix things in life that need mending.

Knowing when it is time to move on is difficult for many people, including myself. I am not an expert on relationships but I do know that you can be happier in life if you look inside and fix that first. Then the people in your life will like you better; hopefully. And if they do not like you better; it may be time to move on.

Your window of living life full of love and hope

Take a long breath; breathing in this water scene and feeling the serenity and calmness it brings to you. Look at the tiny bits of color in the picture and breathe in the greens; the color of life

Which road do you take?

When with your friends do you play together like a couple of frogs? Or do you take turns telling each other about all of your problems?

And when you are with your partner, do you muddle along complaining about life and not stopping to see how much beauty there is in being with someone who loves and cares for you?

Or maybe you are just bored with life, finding that you no longer have anything in common with your partner; maybe they did not give you enough attention, or it is it a mutual exchange of ignoring because you do not like each other anymore.

Do you think that those answers would be enough if it was a business partner? No, you would have to struggle to find answers to your difficulties.

Breaking Up

Whatever the case, it doesn't matter whose fault it is if you are not doing well with your present relationships, it may take a lot of time and effort to make it flow again.

This is where *the rubber meets the road*; the place where you have to ask yourself if it is worth the struggle. And I believe that in some cases it is worth the struggle, and together you can make the relationship stronger and full of love and hope.

Even weeds can look beautiful on a sunny day

The Bond of love

Trees, separate and unable to change, but together they shade each other

And like an infant bonds to its mother almost instantaneously, so do couples.

If you do not have a strong bond; the relationship may move down a separate path. The bonding period for an infant only takes a few hours; but the bonding of adults may take years; where there is the honeymoon stage of romance, the building stage of trust and acceptance and the final stage of respect and honesty. When relationships do not have these ingredients, there are many difficulties and powerful struggles. It becomes a bad recipe without all the ingredients!

And how do you know if you are bonded well enough? You stick together, literally! Did you ever notice people and how they stand next to each other? Truly bonded people stand side by side at a close distance; they do not walk behind each other or separate when they approach others.

What Happened to being honest and giving respect to your partner?

In relationships, some people hold onto grudges; seething silently and then bursting through the seams. They have been mad at their partner for years and never told them. Then they decide to confide in someone else on how terrible life is, and if this someone else is the opposite sex, things may begin to brew because *the grass is always greener on the other side of the fence.* Of course your new love will side and bond with you; making it easier to let go and get divorced, but the problem is still there because there are so much *green grass* in life.

And even if you forgive your partner's infidelity; without respect and honesty, there will always be a dark area in the togetherness that is not spoken of.

Most of the people whom I have spoken to on the longevity of their relationship tell me that the thing that kept the together for so long was respect for the other person, and when you show respect, your partner begins to truly respect you too; giving you the things that you need like the toilet seat put back down.

Balancing Life

Many people give up on relationships because they cannot stand the imbalanced years when one party may be struggling with physical or mental problems and the saying *for better or for worse* become a daily struggle. *I want to be strong as I age, but maybe someday someone will need to care for me and I cannot stand the thought,* said my mother when they put my nana in a nursing home. These issues down the road can break that bond in a marriage.

You build your fort and I will build mine, and together we can build a stronger one that will still be standing when we are not

Until death?

It would be wonderful to be with each other until the end; helping and loving the person who always took care of you. You built your relationship on solid ground, and it took many stones and lumber to make it stand so very long.

I want a relationship like that; the one that everyone is envious about because they never had it; the long standing, kind, caring and trusting love of their lives.

I did not know what I was looking for in a relationship; they just happened, and people will come in and out of your life, most without your control

I am beginning to believe that had I a plan of what I truly wanted out of a relationship, I would have one that is perfect right now; not only my love relationships, but my parents, sisters and friends.

Life is not perfectly planned and your friends may have also changed throughout the years due to your own actions or the fact that you may not have anything in common with them anymore.

People come in and out of your life, and until you understand that sometimes you really do not have anything to do with what continues in your life and what does not; you will be baffled when someone walks out the door and does not return.

I don't remember the last day that my mother lived in her home before she moved to a nursing home but I am sure she felt lost that day; wondering why she could not stay in the home she had spent most of her adult life in.

As we get older it seems that we become attached to certain material things in life like our homes, and it is better not to go that route in life.

I find the best way is less. When you learn how to live with less, things become simple and there are not as many worries about what will happen to you when it is your time to go; you may even pick out your own rest home!

Treasure each moment and each step that you take in life because you only have the here and now.

Do not look too far back, or ahead of yourself; stay in the moment you have right now and live it meaningfully.

Your path will emerge and then you will begin to see why you are here and where you are going.

The simple paths in life are amazing

Ways to be kind to each other, even when it is about to end

Time to sit and go over some of the good things that happened in your lives

The most difficult time in my life was ending my last relationship; walking out without a second thought was what I wanted to do, and that would have been the easier way. But the more difficult way of ending any relationship is to have a long talk with the person; maybe even finding some common ground in that lost love that is not coming back. I remember standing out in a bank parking lot; it was the last time I spoke to my husband, and I wanted to talk longer but he was in a hurry to move on. We struggled for a moment trying to be nice, and then I said, "I guess this is the way it end," Like strangers we walked away. I looked back, not sure if he did. The story does not end there because conversations on the phone continued for quite a few months on the distribution of funds, kids and their support and of course the paperwork that says one of you just could not stand to be with the other.

And when it was said and done I got another phone call a few months later and he was crying, "I want to tell you that my mom died." I started crying too. I was on the phone in another parking lot crying with him for more than an hour.

And I felt the loss of a mother too that day and I wondered why he decided that I was the one to comfort him on that day, but I accepted it, and to this day feel honored that he chose me to cry with. I am sure that he also cried with his new loved one but it felt good to know that I was also included as a member of the family.

There were no more exchanges of being nice except for coming back to our home snow blowing after a major storm, and painting the living room because he had promised to do it years ago. He also wanted to install a sink in the upstairs bathroom but I drew the line at painting. It was getting very difficult seeing him that much after the break-up. To this day I wonder why he helped me so much at the end. Was it out of some love that was tied up deep down inside of him, or was it just guilt?

Even to this day my ex-husband still finds his way to be involved in my life; and as painful as it is I accept it. The latest accomplishment he has made is to raise our granddaughter. He enlisted me in part of the care once a week but that did not last because I said a few things he did not like about his new wife. It is a loss to me not seeing my granddaughter as much, but I accept that too because there is absolutely nothing I can do about it.

Do you find yourself wanting more out of your present day relationships with your partner? If you do, you have to change your attitude to one of a person who is hopeful about right now; not yesterday or tomorrow. Right now you have to begin believing that things can get better.

Hopeful Living

Hope circles around, spinning its warmth and kindness, telling you to hold on tight and never give up. Relationships that include hopefulness, faithfulness, honesty and kindness seem to last the longest.

Sometimes there are choices; the road straight ahead or the one that may have a challenging curve to it taking you to a different place

Hope can give you inspiration and motivation to hold on to your dreams and make them a reality. Sometimes I give up too soon on some of the things I really want to accomplish and the next time I do something new, I remind myself of this so that my staying power is longer. You need stick-*to-it-ness it* in order to accomplish your goals in life.

Teaching yourself how to be more hopeful

Hope is a learning process that takes time to acquire. Hopeful moments, minutes, hours and then hopeful days! Before you know it, you are hopeful about everything in life, and that can help you to be more resilient and happier about your progress toward your goals in life, and your new found ability to help others gather their hopeful moments.

Helping others

This new found strength you have acquired in hopeful living can help you and others too. You can bring hope to a dismal moment in someone's life by giving a needed hug or a pat on the back to someone in need along with honoring yourself and your accomplishment in life because you had the staying power of hopefulness. People begin to seek you out for your *hopeful signs* that help them to change themselves to more abundant life that is full of love and harmony.

Success in life

Hopefulness and a positive attitude can add to your chances of success. I practice hopeful moments all day long, and I enlist others to do the same by stopping them from continuing down a path of gloom and doom. I can feel the energy around someone who is positive and it is good, but the energy around negative people keeps me at a distance. Those negative vibrations surrounding negatively spirited people can roll onto you.

What is hope?

Hope is not just about attitude or being persistent, hope is about that deep feeling inside where your sprit brings you moments of awe. You have to live the dream; really feeling hope inside your spirit; hanging on to it no matter what happens. Remember that you have choice in every moment to change your attitude, mood and emotion to a more positive moment in time that is filled with hope, wonder and love.

The most beautiful flowers have thorns

Flowers can be beautiful to gaze at, especially in the spring when the flowering trees bloom with their sweet smelling scents. The flowers that I picked today were soft and white with a yellow center, and their delicate blossoms were falling off so I had to carefully pick them. And these flower had some thorns like a rose that guarded their preciousness. I was not surprised by their thorns because later on in the summer, they are the bushes that have dark purple berries that my grandchildren love to pick and eat. Those precious flowers and berries need some protection. You too may have some thorns from past happenings that guard you from experiencing true happiness and love but you still have time for some happiness and love in your life.

Happiness is your internal bliss. Hope, happiness and harmony go together internally keeping you on the positive side of life, and they are all there for you in different ways, you just have to *let your thorns and precious flowers be seen by others.*

Being more positive

When you have a negative thought that you need to rid yourself of begin to think of a musical harmony that is soothing to lull you out of the negative moment, or if you are bold; sing and allow your own voice to put a smile on your face.

I love to listen to the birds singing in my yard each morning; their songs are harmonious and loving. They too have internal bliss that keeps them happy and content.

Loving Nature

If you can find a way to be happy, do it right now because you do not want regret later on when you think about how different life could have been if only you were happier.

The two most important things in life are happiness and love.

When you have love around you, there is harmony.

And for happiness, you have to create it. Be creative today and decide promptly that you are going to be happy no matter what.

Of course sad things will happen to you, and you will have to grieve and get through the difficult times, but happiness is like hope, it floats back up to you and tells you it is time to move on. Try to bring fresh flowers into your home each day, and smell them as you pass them by; this will be your happy moment for the day; reminding you that you are on this Earth for only a short time, *so stop and smell the roses*. Like the sweet sounds of a musical melody, you can be happy, hopeful and full of harmony.

Hope Floats Just Like a Boat

When I think of what I am hopeful about I begin to remember how strong hope can be. There have been many studies done on hopeful and optimistic people, and what hope does to you is amazing.

I tend to my garden well, hoping it will be a beautiful one every year

Hope can help you to live longer; in fact hopeful, optimistic people are here on this Earth longer, spreading their joy and love to others.

Float your boat

When I say that hope floats like a boat; hope stays with you for the long road ahead. The more hopeful you are, the more successful you become. You are floating on top of the world, passing along this optimistic view of life to others.

Make your life as green as your garden

Green is an amazing color, and in the spring and summer when the Earth is covered with the greens of nature; breathe it in and love the color. Green helps to change your mood; bringing in sunshine even on cloudy days.

In Pauline Wills book entitled: *Color Therapy: The Use of Colour for Healing and Health* she describes green as neither hot or cold but a powerful balance of harmony and sympathy which can bring about powerful negative and positive energy; bringing about balance to one's life because you need both to create wholeness.

Color Therapy and Cancer

There continues to be much research on the use of color and plants used to help with cancer tumors. Recently, garlic has been in the news on its power in ridding toxins from the body.

And Barry Lynes in his book *The Healing of Cancer* describes the work of green for cancer therapy; he and Dr. William Kelly have shown that green light can destroy cancer cells especially with its complementary color magenta.

Color for healing and Cancer therapy source: Wills, P. (1993). Color Therapy: *The Use of Colour for Health and Healing*. Element. Rockport, MA.

Hope Helps with Strength

Wherever you path has taken you, I hope it has been filled with love.

This was my path as a child, a rocky beach road. I sat on the edge of this cliff on most days watching the waves roll in and out, sometimes rough waters stopped me from sitting, but I still stood strong.

Hope is always there no matter what you say or do; you can bring hope back into your life with just a change of attitude deep inside your spirit. You can be hopeful even when things look bleak; your *hope status* is up to you. Everything gets old. Some metals turn to rust and we get rusty too. Hope can bring you back to your center; balancing out any negativity with some positive and hopeful ideas that can help you with happiness and success.

Creative Moments

My hopeful ideas have become creative words that I bring to everyone in my daily writings; pressing on, staying calm and carrying on no matter what. Reach for hope when you need it because you do not have much choice but to carry on, and you cannot change anything that is already set in stone. Acceptance may be your only hope.

Everything unfolds the way it is supposed to

Let things unfold without struggling all the time because everything plays out the way it is supposed to no matter how much you struggle trying to change it. You only have control over yourself and cannot change anyone else, because that person has to change themselves.

I spent many years hoping to change someone's behavior; believing that if I persisted and struggled, the person would stop drinking. It took me many years to figure out that I could not control anyone's behavior except for my own, and now I begin there with my own behaviors that I want or hope to change.

Times that are not ideal help you to grow stronger

Your life will be filled with good and bad times, and no matter what you do everything unfolding the way it is supposed to. Even metal changes color or turns rusty and can or cannot be cleaned and re-used. You can clean yourself up and become stronger; like a shiny piece of green glass that has been tumbled by waves from the ocean. When you press on in a hopeful way you survive many tragic happenings; becoming stronger and carrying on.

Relationship Lessons: number one and two

Always bring fresh flowers into your home

Number 1: Stop blaming yourself for past difficulties

Number 2: Nothing is a mistake; everything is a lesson

There have been so very many changes in my life that I have a hard time remembering them all.

As time passing me by, I begin to think of some of the changes as lessons not mistakes.

You learn from each mistake (lesson) that you make, and hope you will live a full life full of happiness and love.

When you make a mistake, it is like a guide for you so that you do not do it again, and if you do, that is alright too because life is full of mishaps and misunderstandings.

Perfection

So what if you do not do something exactly right! Does everything in life have to be perfectly done? Are you looking for the perfect person, or a person who is just like you with flaws and imperfections?

No one has a perfect relationship no matter what they tell you

They may have a loving relationship that is thriving but it does not mean that there have been no mistakes made. It all comes down to what you are able to accept in life from another person. Some people are more tolerant of problems; others get out of relationships at the drop of a hat!

Where do you stand?

I stand with imperfection. I do not want a person in my life who thinks they know everything or are smarter than everyone else. I want mistakes made and imperfections to show on the outside; even if it is embarrassing. I remember embarrassing moments in my life, and I want my partner to tell me about their mishaps!

Putting things away

I do not ponder on mistakes anymore, even if someone asks me about my past, I do not give detailed answers that stir me up. Things in the past should stay there. I would much rather think of the past in my child's mind where I was always up in a tree looking down at the world. I loved climbing and still do. I also road a bike a lot as a child; and still do. Those good memories stick with you, and guide you through your life. And those bad moments need to stay in the past. Nothing is a mistake. Every difficulty is a learning experience that pays you forward in some way later on. Everything in life unfolds as it should even the problems and mistakes in life become a way to practice life's lessons.

Learning how to relax and "just breathe" is a great goal in life!

Sit and breathe in patience and gratitude; breathing out discontentment

Love Lost

Going back to where I grew up reminds me that things do pass along and you have to let go of your past and concentrate on where you are right now

Look back on your life and find some times when you felt *as if* you were in love forever, because it was never supposed to end. And then think of yourself wherever you are right now and begin to think about a number. The number 1-10 of where you are on the *love scale* now. Perhaps trying to recapture what you think you may have missed or maybe in a romantic relationship now that you cherish.

If you are older, you will know that loving relationships do change; some of them for the better, and some not so much. But don't let yourself dwell in the past too long because you have not lost anything, you have changed the way you look at things in life, and that is wonderful.

Attitude

It is all about your attitude as you age, not so much about romantic love and the fairy tale endings.

In the spring of life, the flowers are colorful and full if you tend to them well

People live, find their way through life and then pass on just as you plant your garden in the springtime, tending to it well. And the garden flourishes. The same philosophy on relationships; if you tend to them, they flourish, and if not, their do not do so well. I would love to believe that I have tended to all of my relationships in life. I know that I have strong children and grandchildren who are growing up with love in their hearts. I have passed through some romantic relationships that were not tended to enough to stay strong and stable. And now, I persist on with love in my heart and a *special rake* in my hands to tend to my gardening, weeding it well.

Respect in Relationships

Allow your relationships to evolve like a butterfly; starting out slowly and becoming beautiful

RESPECT

Reason with each other

Explain clearly what you mean

Settle down before you speak

Pause and listen, do not ignore your partner,

Examine your relationship regularly for insight

Create a caring, loving environment for each other

Talk to each other about important and not so important things!

Respect in relationships

Respect is letting the person know that you feel they have contributed to your life in many ways, and telling this special person about it every time it passes through your mind. Not just on birthdays, and other celebrations; respect comes in different ways from a simple thank you to being there for your partner through difficult times, and not embarrassing them in front of others; sticking side by side through the good and bad; problems and heartaches. Keeping your relationship fresh and alive takes hard work; building, honoring and respecting your partner is the given but sometimes you may forget about this as the relationship ages, taking advantage of your partner's good nature, or for whatever reason such as leaning on them too much. When you respect someone, you usually get it back. It is so important to any relationship, not only marriage.

As a connected relationship ages, some people begin to take advantage of their partner in many ways, and this may draw them apart instead of together. If you have been through quite a few relationships already, you know when the Honey Moon is over, and you may begin to ignore, disrespect or build up some anger toward your spouse. This is where the problems may have begun, and you both may have started to separate because of disrespect and planned ignoring.

And it seems that once things have gone on for a long time, it is like a snowball rolling down a hill very fast, picking up more and more snow; becoming larger and larger as time goes on.

How to fix broken parts

There may be reason to turn the clocks back and take a look at what brought you together to see whether or not it is worth fixing, and mending takes a long time; stitch by stitch you can grow back together, but it has to be with both parties sharing the *mending ways* for it to work. If you agree and want to try to mend your relationship before it falls apart, I applaud your efforts because many things in life are worthy to pursue and the efforts may make your love for each other even stronger and more balanced.

After the rain

Did you ever notice that after a rain there is a sweet smell of clean?

First tomato of the season

The Earth cleanses itself as we do in different ways. I believe that after some of my relationships ended it took a lot of time to cleanse myself of the negativity and replace it with some positive living, thinking and loving. It was a long haul, and still, every single time I think about the past, I cannot believe it happened. I truly believed in happily ever after, but for most part, when the happy part ends so does the relationship.

Why is it easier to grow plants?

Gardening is not easy. It takes a lot of tending, watering and weeding to create a beautiful garden. When you grow things lovingly; the relationships that you create with nature stays loving and in harmony as long as you care for yourself and your plants.

It is like a spiritual awakening where you become one with your plants. They grow, and you reap the benefits of a garden well-tended; its beauty is amazing and every day you can sit and breathe in the wonderful colors of nature.

Tending to Relationships

And with relationships, there is much tending to the garden of life; and if you do not cleanse and clear out the bad; the good things will never be because it becomes overgrown with weeds that are very difficult to manage. A good place to start may be with being kinder than you have been to your partner, even when they are not kind. This is the first step because eventually they will come around to treating you as you treat them.

Happiness helps you to grow strong and centered

Another important step in any relationship is to find a way to be happy! Your internal bliss circles its energy to others, and rubs off. Find a way to be as happy as possible and things will change for you, and for those around you. The people who begin to circle around you will reap the benefits of your positive energy and love.

Tears can be Healing

I have tears today because it is close to my mom's birthday

When I am feeling lost and alone, pink flowers help me to smile

I have been thinking a lot about what it will be like, and it is difficult thinking about her all the time. Yesterday, I thought I heard her voice as I walked down the street. She called my name and I turned around but did not see anything except the rustle of a small tree branch that had fallen from a nearby pink flowering tree that has tiny flowers that fall ever so softly like snowflakes.

I wonder if it will be different when a year has passed since my mom has died because all the authorities on grief and sorrow agree that it takes at least a year before you can move on. And moving on is never without tears at moments least expected because the loss will always be with you, letting you know that the person is still there inside of you, telling you that they are okay. And the childhood memories keep flooding back with my mom near me, telling me it's time for dinner, or standing at the end of the driveway waiting with me for the bus, or sweeping the driveway when I returned from school. I have been trying to figure out why I keep having these childhood memories of my mother, but I guess it is part of the healing process.

Joy

Think of the word joy when you feel sad because it can help you to feel the love that is deep down inside of your spiritual being. And your spirit can help you with the healing that you need to do when you are feeling lonely and tearful.

Having people around you can help with healing

Sometimes I feel like I will never heal from my losses, but then a person in my life touches me, giving me a hug or a gentle smile that brings me back to the present. As you age there will be more and more losses, and many of the losses you have felt in the past may not compare to the losses you are feeling right now. But the good news is that those smaller loses, like the death of your cat help prepare you for the bigger loses such as the death of your mother. Mom is still with me when I need her and I can feel her leaning on me sometimes. She wraps herself around my shoulders and gives me a great big hug, and it always helps me to know she is still near.

Love and Hope

Yellow; a warm soothing color to breathe in

When you are angry, sad, upset or frustrated, and you cannot shake it, those emotions cause difficulty in your mind, body and soul. I know that when I am upset or angry, I eat too much, stay in the negative moment and then I feel bad for quite some time. I might yell at someone, walk around with a frown and think I am the only one who has problems! And when you begin to see that there are much greater difficulties in the world then your own; you will put a smile on your face and gather some hope and love.

Hope

And when I am in a hopeful spirit, things just seem to unfold in a nice way; the day becomes one beautiful moment after another. Hope and optimism can be practiced daily to get you used to this state of mind.

Love

And Love is an emotion that comes from inside, inviting you into its glory. Love is in your soul, waiting for you to bring it to the surface so that you can be happy and find pleasure in being alive. Just look at nature and you will begin to see what the love of creation means to you. And then look at small children with their eyes full of fun and sparkle, and begin to think and act as they do; so carefree and loving; always in the moment, never thinking ahead or behind. Children are natural mindful beings.

The wonders of the green of the Earth

Think of each day as a gift that you can share with others. Give the gift of a warm smile to someone you do not know today. Give the gift of a flower to the first child you see today, and give the gift of saying; *hello, how are you?* to a dear friend you have not spoken to in some time. These gifts that you give can be a simple way to bring love and hope to yourself and others.

Tiger Lilies for mom

I put some flowers on your grave today for your birthday. You always had a beautiful sunny day for your birthday, and today is no exception. It is going to be one of the hottest days of the summer this year, and you enjoyed sunshiny, hot days.

When I breathe in the color orange it energizes my soul

I chose tiger lilies from my garden; 3 of them for each of your children.

Tiger lilies are so strong they grow like weeds. And you too were stronger than anyone I have ever met. You met challenges on a daily basis gracefully. You honored every breath that you took in life; explaining to me that you will never die. And you are here now to guide me in writing about you and your wonder.

According too many theories on color, the color orange is the color of love and happiness. I believe that is why I chose these beautiful flowers for you. You brought love and happiness to my childhood, and helped me through many struggles in my life without telling me what to do. You stood by all of your children no matter what the circumstances. I only hope that I am treasured by my children as much as you are by your family. No unkind words were ever spoken of you. You were like your name; an angel in disguise. And now you have your wings and can send your energy to everyone who misses you.

Missing you is like a deep hole in my soul. There is a spot down there that is beginning to fill with the energy you send me to keep writing about you and your life. You want everyone to know that you are still here and speak to us in different ways; it may be in the soft breezes that circle around dropping scents of purple, soft lilacs, or just the scattering of leaves in front of me as l walk along my path. And I know it is you, and as I breathe in the warm, fresh air, I think of you every moment of the day.

Love and happiness theories on Color: Wills, P. (1993). *Colour Therapy: The Use of Color for Healing and Health*. Element. Rockport, MA.

Tiger Lillies by my Window

 Find your way through life embracing each moment and remember that life is full of one beautiful moment after another.

Doris

www.ingramcontent.com/pod-product-compliance
Lightning Source LLC
Chambersburg PA
CBHW042114040426
42448CB00003B/270